ABU SIMBEL

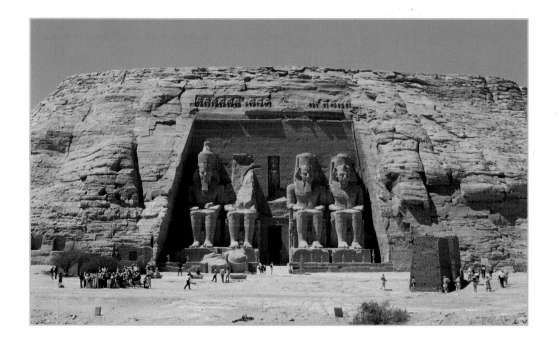

Text by Giovanna Magi

THE HISTORY OF THE TEMPLES
AND THEIR RESCUE

BONECHI

History

Some three hundred kilometres from Aswan, in the region of Nubia, lying almost on the border with Sudan, is a strikingly beautiful and majestic monument built by the most powerful pharaoh in the history of Egypt: the temple of Abu Simbel, in theory dedicated to the deities **Amon-Ra**, **Harmakhis** and **Ptah**, but actually erected for the eternal glorification of **Ramses II** himself.

Abu Simbel is not just one of the most beautiful temples in Egypt – it is certainly the most unusual and imposing – but is also symbolic of the vast enterprise undertaken to save the 14 temples of Nubia that were threatened by the rising waters of Lake Nasser.

The fact that the temple would be submerged by the lake was a danger that alarmed the entire world. And while Abu Simbel was the most beautiful and impressive of the Nubian temples, it was also the most difficult to save given the material from which it was made, its location and the design of its structure. Despite the problems, however, sheer determination and the wonders of technology combined to achieve one of the most incredible feats of dismantelling and reconstruction ever undertaken by archaeologists, thus saving the temple and perpetuating its memory throughout the centuries.

AMON RA

The Theban priesthood assimilated the sun-god Ra to Amon-Ra, represented in anthropomorphic form with a tiara decorated with two tall feathers. The name is derived from the root "imn" meaning "to hide". Thebes was the main city of the deity's cult. The heretics from Amarna, followers of the the revolutionary king, Akhenaton, rebelled against Amon and his priests and introduced the monotheistic cult of Aton, but on the death of this schismatic monarch, the Theban priests, never entirely suppressed, re-established the old religion and deities.

HARMAKHIS

A sun god and keeper of the gates to the other world, portrayed in the form of a sphinx, Harmakhis is the Greek version of Hor-em-Akhet, meaning "Horus of the horizon", and was used to design the sphinx of Giza.

PTAH

Considered the creator of the world, Ptah is the oldest of the gods and is patron of artists. The most important deity of Memphis, he is represented as a mummy, with a close-fitting headdress, hands outside the shroud and holding a composite sceptre. The root of the name is "pth" meaning "to give form".

Originally this black granite bust Ramses II was part of a statue found in a temple on the Delta and later re-used in the large temple Tanis, where it was found by Auguste Ferdinand Mariette in 1863. The monarch is represented here as a youth, wearing a rounded headdress mounted by a uraeus, a broad collar band and finely pleated clothing.
(The Cairo Egyptian Museum).

Ybsambul

It is a strange fact that Abu Simbel, now considered one of the most famous monuments of Egypt, was almost totally unknown even as late as the 19th century. Ybsambul had become little more than a legend. The story of the site begins on 22 March 1813 when Johann Ludwig Burckhardt, a Swiss historian, known to the Arabs as Ibrahim ibn Abdallah, landed on this bank of the Nile accompanied by the local guide Saad to visit the temple of Nefertari, convinced that the temple dedicated to the

Giovanni Battista Belzoni

beautiful and adored wife of the pharaoh was the only antiquity of Abu Simbel. He was just about to climb back up the sandy slope "... when by a lucky chance I took a few steps further to the south and my eyes fell on what is still visible of four colossal statues, cut from the rock." The strong wind had blown the sand dozens of metres down the gorge, heaping it ever higher against the enormous stone giants and leaving only part of the heads exposed. The blanket of sand left them barely visible and it was impossible for Burckhardt to tell if the statues were standing or

Johann Ludwig Burckhardt

sitting. Abu Simbel, the mythical Ybsambul, had, however, been rediscovered. Just four years later, on 1 August 1817, another adventurer, **Giovanni Battista Belzoni**, the most daring of them all, managed to remove the sand from the upper part of a doorway and discover the entrance. After eleven centuries a European was to break into the architectural masterpiece and personal achievement of Ramses the Great. Following Belzoni, many travellers faced the discomfort and uncertainties of crossing the Nubian desert to arrive at Abu Simbel; all were impressed by the magnificence of the monument and all were moved by the sudden appearance of the gigantic, imposing figures that seemed to emerge from the sand for some fantastic, supernatural event. Scholars too, arrived: the Italians Ippolito Rosellini and Salvatore Cherubini, the French artist, Nestor L'Hôte, François Champollion who wrote that this temple alone made the journey into Nubia worthwhile, the German archaeologist Heinrich Schliemann who had discovered entire cities such as Troy, Mycenae and Tiryns and described the site as

David Roberts arrived in Abu Simbel in December 1838 and, having moored his boat, he remained there for some time during which he painted this watercolour showing a general view of the temples, separated by an immense cascade of sand.

"the most powerful work of art in the world". Once the sand had been entirely removed from the façade of the temple, visitors could enter more easily, without fear of finding the entrance suddenly blocked again. At last it was possible to fully appreciate the beauty and complex design of the rock-cut temple of Abu Simbel.

In his diary, Giovanni Battista Belzoni described the moment of entering the Great Temple of Abu Simbel: "The sand, heaped up against the rock that dominates the temple by the wind coming from the north, had gradually encroached across the façade and buried the entrance by three quarters. Thus the first time that I approached the temple I lost hope of freeing the entrance as it seemed quite impossible to reach the doorway. ... The sand was slipping across from one side to the other of the façade and consequently it was pointless to try to open a straight access towards the entrance; it was thus necessary to excavate in the opposite direction so that the sand fell beyond the façade. ... The morning of the first of August we went to the temple very early, excited by the idea of finally entering the underground chambers that we had uncovered. ... We stepped into the passage we had opened and had the pleasure of being the first to descend into the largest and most beautiful underground chamber in Nubia, and to examine a monument comparable to the most beautiful in all of Egypt. ... We were at first astonished by the immensity of the place; we found magnificent antiquities, paintings, sculptures and massive statues."

A panoramic view of the two temples at Abu Simbel, rebuilt above Lake Nasser.

The rock-cut temple of Abu Simbel

The temple of Abu Simbel is an exact transferral of the architectural form of an Egyptian inner sanctuary temple cut deep inside the rock.

Sculpted into the mountain, the façade is 38 metres long and 31 high. This is framd by a convex 'torus' moulding, and is surmounted by

rnice with uraei (the sacred asp) above which
carved a row of 22 seated baboons, each two
d a half metres high. Below the torus
oulding is a cornice engraved with dedicatory
eroglyphics, and in a niche below this in the

middle of the façade is a large high-relief statue
representing **Ra-Harakhti** with a falcon's head,
flanked by two low-relief figures of Ramses II.
Four colossal statues of Ramses II seated form
the supporting columns of the façade. Even on

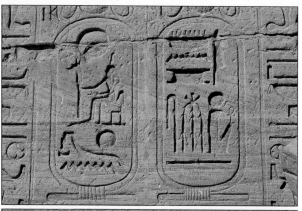

The Great Temple of Abu Simbel is also noted for its rich decoration: above, the cartouches with the name of the pharaoh, images of Africans and Asians taken prisoner by Ramses II, and statues of Horus.

this monumental scale they reproduce the true features of the monarch. They are 20 metres high and measure more than 4 from ear to ear, while the lips, measuring over a metre, express a soft, gentle smile. The pharaoh is represented with his hands resting in his lap, wearing the double crown and a headdress with deep folds on either side of his face. The second statue on the left is broken and part of the head and body lie on the ground. Beside and between the legs

Ramses II is always portrayed with an expression of great serenity in the temple of Abu Simbel. On discovery, Burckhardt described it thus, "The face of the head that emerged from the sands was the most expressive, youthful countenance, approaching nearer to the Grecian model of beauty than that of any ancient Egyptian figure I have seen".

Below, the row of twenty-two sitting baboons above the cornice of the façade.

Ra-Harakhti

This deity is the supreme personification of the sun and was especially venerated in Heliopoli. The composite form of Ra-Harakhti combines the three various forms of Khepri, Ra and Atum (the rising sun, midday sun and setting sun). The form is anthropomorphic, with a falcon's head, and bears the solar disc. During the fifth dynasty the deity became associated with Amon and became the most important god, Amon-Ra.

So that he could paint the exterior of the temple in its entirety, David Roberts set his easel up on the mountain of sand piled in front of the façade. During a break in his work the English artist climbed over the monumental statues so that he could study the decorations in greater detail. Roberts noticed that the figures were considerably damaged and in his diary deplored the way in which "tourists from the London suburbs and yankee travellers" had removed fragments of the feet and hands of the statues.

of each colossus are other statues representing members of the royal family including a daughter (who was also his wife) Bent'anat, his mother Tuya, his wife Nefertari, his son Amenhirkhopshef, and another daughter and wife, Merytamun. On the base and along the sides of the seats are figures of African and Asiatic prisoners. A "multitude of workers imprisoned by his sword" worked on the monumental façade under the orders of Pyay, head of all the sculptors, as we read inside the temple. The work of the sculptors was followed by that of the painters for, at the time of Ramses, the temple was most probably richly painted and decorated.

The interior

From the blinding light of day one passes to the interior where the shadowy light emphasises the mysterious and evocative atmosphere. The pronaos is a vast rectangular hall 18 metres long and 16.70 wide. This is flanked by eight Osiris pillars ten metres tall arranged in two rows, representing Osiris with the features of Ramses. The colossi on the left wear the white crown of Upper Egypt, those on the right, the "pschent" or double crown. Their arms, crossed over their chests, hold the sceptre and flail. Decorating the roof of the central nave is the great vulture of the goddess Nekhbet, protrectress of Upper Egypt, while the aisles on either side are painted with stars.

Left, a view of the entrance hall and below, the fresco of the pharaoh, between two gods, including the god Min, represented as ithyphallix, with two tall feathers on his head and his arm raised to grasp the flail.

"We entered the hall which is fifty seven feet long and fifty two feet wide, supported by a colonnade of square pilasters. Each pilaster is sculpted with a figure; their heads reaching the roof, these caryatids, similar to those of Medinet Habu, are extremely well-made and are little damaged by time. Their pedestals measure five and a half square feet and are engraved with fine hieroglyphs as too are the walls, in a style which is superior to and certainly more lively than normal Egyptian hieroglyphs both in their execution and choice of subject. They describe battles, attacks on fortified castles, triumphs over the Ethiopians, sacrifices etc. ... Some of the columns have been broken by the heat in the enclosed atmosphere, heat that during our visit was still so great that the thermometer would have exceeded one hundred and thirty degrees had the fluid been able to rise that high."

(Giovanni Battista Belzoni, *Journeys in Egypt and Nubia*.)

The frescoes in the Great Temple of Abu Simbel always represent the pharaoh flanked by various divinities.
Facing page, below right, a detail of two Osiris pilasters where the pharaoh is wearing the crown of Upper Egypt.

The Sanctuary and the "miracle of the sun"

Sixty-five metres from the entrance, deep in the heart of the mountain, is the sanctuary, the most intimate and secret part of the temple, a small room four metres by seven. Here sits the statue of the deified Ramses II together with the triad of Ptah, Amon-Ra and Harmakhis.

It was obvious ever since discovery in the 19th century that nothing in this temple was left to chance and that it was built according to a very precise logic and pre-established plan.

François Champollion was the first of several scholars to note what has become known as the "miracle of the sun".

Abu Simbel was built along a pre-determined axis: twice a year, corresponding to the equinoxes, the rising sun penetrates the heart of the mountain and illuminates the statues in the sanctuary. The first rays of the sun follow the axis of the temple precisely, crossing its entire length and gradually flooding the statues of Amon, Harmakhis and the pharaoh in light.

It takes about twenty minutes for the light to pass, yet remarkably Ptah is never struck by the sun's rays: Ptah is, in fact, the god of darkness and the dead.

THE BATTLE OF KADESH IN THE POEM OF PENTAUR

The wall decorations in the Great Temple of Abu Simbel celebrate the military victories of Ramses II. The most interesting and famous is on the north wall where one can follow the various phases of the **Battle of Kadesh** which concluded the pharaoh's military campaign against the Hittites in the summer of 1275 BC. The *Poem* of Pentaur – though Pentaur was probably not the author, but the scribe who copied it down – is a celebratory, but also objective account of the pharaoh's courage and triumph and recounts with great accuracy the characteristic images of battle: bodies that are fallen and heaped one on top of another, smashed heads, hands chopped off and the pharaoh upright in his chariot, head protected by the "khepresh", a bow held taut by his powerful arm. This long epic poem was engraved in hieroglyphics not only here in Abu Simbel but also on the walls of the temples of Luxor, Karnak, Ramesseum and Derr.

Ramses II seizes an enemy by the hair: this is a typical example of how the victorious king is portrayed in Egyptian iconography.

Although Seti I, Ramses' father, had conquered the Hittites at Kadesh, the victory had not been sufficiently decisive and in the spring of the fifth year of his reign, Ramses decided to resolve the thorny problem of Syria once and for all.
First he reinforced the army adding a fourth division to the three already existing: Amon, Ptah, Ra and Seth, each consisting of 5,000 men. His personal guard was formed by "sherden", "warriors from the sea without masters", probably pirates from the coasts of Asia Minor. Ramses' army was equipped with war chariots that the Egyptians had inherited from the invasion of Hyksos and had then skillfully improved making them speedier and lighter. The cart had a charioteer and soldier with bow and arrow; the harness of the two horses at the neck and breast permitted great ease of handling. With 20,000 men and 200 war chariots, on the ninth day of the second month of summer, 1275 BC, Ramses II moved out of Egypt. Following the same strategy as Tutmos III, he followed the Gaza strip as far as Canaan, proceeded through Galilee as far as the source of the Jordan, finally arriving in the broad valley of Bequaa extending between the mountains of Lebanon and the southern reaches of Syria. A month after leaving Egypt, Ramses camped ten kilometres from the city of Kadesh, a Hittite stronghold on the river Orontes. The Hittite king, Muwatalli had created a powerful coalition here with an army of 40,000 men and some 2,500 war chariots.
Both sides were aware that the battle of Kadesh would be decisive for control of the entire territory of Syria and Palestine.
The capture of two Bedouin deserters from the Hittite army and their false information regarding the enemy's movements lead Ramses to

believe that Muwatalli was more that one hundred kilometres to the north of Kadesh. The pharaoh fell for the trick and with only the Amon division, crossed the river and the forest of Robawi until he was in sight of the city of Kadesh.

Unexpectedly the Hittites, who were in fact close to the eastern side of the city, attacked, taking the Ra Division by surprise as it marched directly towards Ramses' camp where he was still discussing the military tactic for the forthcoming battle. While the enemy created confusion and all began to seem lost, the pharaoh threw himself into the fray, leaping onto the chariot with the horseman Menna. Alone, deserted by his soldiers who had been seized by panic, Ramses called on Amon, begging that he would not abandon him and would save his life, "O divine Amon ... You see how I am alone! Are you not my father and am I not your son? I have always done as you have wished ... count the obelisks that I have built in your honour! O Divine Amon, now that I am alone and abandoned by all, my hands and prayers reach out to you. Are you not stronger than a thousand warriors and a thousand heroes?"

And Amon must have heard him, because Ramses – driven by a holy rage – threw himself into the fray wounding and killing numerous enemies, creating confusion in the Hittite ranks and thus making time for the other Egyptian divisions to arrive at the scene of the battle and attack from behind. The Battle of Kadesh also continued the following day and in fact, neither side actually emerged entirely victorious.

The battle was important for two reasons however; firstly because it confirmed Egyptian military power, blocking Hittite expansion, and second because it was the first battle of ancient history to be entirely documented.

Sculpted on the base of one of the colossal statues of Abu Simbel are figures of Nubian prisoners, conquered by the triumphant pharaoh.

Portrayed in this magnificent gold ring, now in the Louvre Museum in Paris, are the two valiant horses that took part in the battle of Kadesh with Ramses, "Victory at Thebes" and "Mut is happy". The pharaoh swore to record that memorable day as follows, " ... I personally will undertake to be present every day when they are given their forage ... in the midst of the battle it was they who were there to save me ... it was they who fought beside me...".

General view of the Temple of Hathor, dedicated to Nefertari: large statues of Ramses II stand at the entrance to the temple.

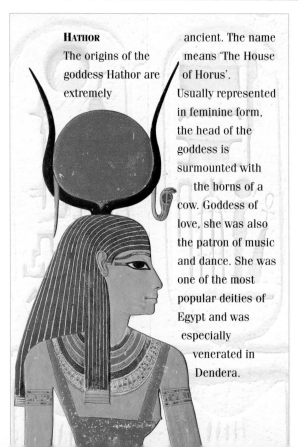

HATHOR

The origins of the goddess Hathor are extremely ancient. The name means 'The House of Horus'. Usually represented in feminine form, the head of the goddess is surmounted with the horns of a cow. Goddess of love, she was also the patron of music and dance. She was one of the most popular deities of Egypt and was especially venerated in Dendera.

The temple of Hathor

Despite appearances, Abu Simbel is more than a monumental self-glorification of Ramses II. One has only to leave the great temple and turn left towards the temple of **Hathor**, dedicated by the pharaoh to his wife, **Nefertari**. The six statues, ten metres tall, each with their left leg set slightly forward, actually seem to emerge from the rock and walk towards the light. Nefertari is represented as Hathor with the horns of the sacred cow, the solar disk and two plumes.

NEFERTARI
"MOST LOVING AND FAIR OF FACE"

Ramses II had eight wives, but the most important and beloved was, without doubt, his first wife, Nefertari, married before he acceded to the throne. Nefertari-Meri-en-Mut ('beloved of Mut') "most loving and fair of face, elegantly bearing the two plumes, gentle in love and Lady of the Two Lands", was possibly descended from the Ay family. As the "First Royal Wife", the main consort of Ramses, it was always she who was by his side at official occasions and religious ceremonies.

Nefertari certainly died before the temple dedicated to her was finished as Bent'anat, daughter of Isinofret, already appears as queen on the third pilaster in the south row of the hall. Above, a portrait of Nefertari painted on a wall of her tomb in the Valley of the Queens, discovered in 1904 by Ernesto Schiaparelli. The pillars and interior of the Small Temple are seen on the left, while the detail on the right shows the head of the goddess above hieroglyphs relating stories of the king and queen.

The divine consecration of the queen is also celebrated in the delightfully simple interior – an almost square chamber with six pilasters in two rows, carved with images of Hathor. Engraved beneath the head of the goddess are stories of Nefertari and Ramses. The walls of this chamber too are decorated with the customary scenes of sacrifice and the massacre of prisoners by the warrior king. The hall leads to a vestibule and beyond to the sanctuary where the pharaoh is represented honouring Hathor, identified as his consort. Set between two pillars, and portrayed in the likeness of the sacred cow, the goddess truly seems to stand away from the rock with particularly striking effect.
It is impossible not to sense in this small temple a most human and tender act of love for his wife by the great pharaoh.

THE RESCUE OF THE TEMPLES

For many centuries the two rock-cut temples of Abu-Simbel on the banks of the Nile were seen not only as a memorial to the power and deification of Ramses II, but as the achievement of an architectural and technical challenge – a challenge that two thousand years later faced engineers and technicians from around the world again. The danger that the temples would be submerged by the waters of Lake Nasser drew global attention and the temple became symbolic of the campaign to save all the monuments of Nubia. Between 10th and 12th June 1963 the Egyptian government gave its final approval to a project that involved complete removal of the entire mass of rock by cutting the temple into blocks and subsequently rebuilding it in a higher location. The rescue operation was immensely complex and involved the organization of thousands of workmen and engineers. The task was also a furious race against time. Work began in April 1964 but already by the end of the summer the waters of the artificial lake had risen more rapidly than expected. Just some figures: 1,036 blocks with an average weight of 30 tons each were moved, while a further 1,112 were cut from the rock around the temples and 33 tons of resin were used to consolidate the rock structure - it was the most incredible project of dismantelling and reconstruction that archaeologists had ever attempted. The two temples were rebuilt on ground 90 metres higher, exactly as before. It was realised however, that straightforward reconstruction was not possible as the weight of

the artificial mountain covering the monument would have crushed it. Two enormous domes of reinforced concrete were therefore built to bear the pressure from the mountain above and so protect the temples like an enormous bell. The backfill was used to cover the concrete domes and the sand itself would rapidly fill in the cracks. Work finished on

Pages 28-32: images of the immense labour involved in dismantling the temples. It was only possible to save these masterpieces of human achievement with international cooperation.

The writer, André Malraux (1901-1976) was French Minister of Culture in 1958 and 1959. Below are some excerpts from his speech to UNESCO at the opening of the global campaign to save the temples of Nubia.

For the first time, on 8th March 1960, precisely at a time when many of them are involved in a secret or declared war, all nations are called upon to save the works of a civilization that belongs to none of them. [...] These magnificent temples were, above all, witnesses, now the only ones that we have inherited from the Ancient Orient: and what witnesses they are, these cataleptic masterpieces that for three thousand years seemed to be united in the same eternal sleep. [...]
The survival of Egypt lies with her art, not with illustrious names or strings of victories. [...] Despite Kadesh, one of the decisive battles in history, despite the cartouches, shattered and newly engraved by order of the intrepid pharaoh eager to impose his descendancy on the gods, Senusret is less known to us today than poor Akhenaton. And our artists are obsessed by the face of queen Nefertiti, just as Cleopatra tormented our poets. But Cleopatra was a queen that has no face, and Nefertiti is a face that has no queen. [...]
For the first time humanity has discovered a universal language of art. [...]
Look, old river whose tides enabled astrologers to establish the most ancient date in history, the men who will move these colossi far from your fertile yet devastating waters are arriving from all over the world. Night falls, and once again you reflect the constellations beneath which Isis performed funerary rituals, the star that Ramses beheld. But even the most humble of the workmen that will save the images of Isis and Ramses will tell you what you have always known but will hear for the first time, "There is only one action over which indifferent stars and unchanging rivers have no sway: it is the action of a man who snatches something from death

2 September 1968 – barely in time
s the waters were already slowly
owing into the enormous,
esolately empty caverns left below.
he vast rock complex above was
ompleted and, as punctually as
ver, in February 1969 the "miracle
f the sun" occurred just as before.
nce again, the rays of the sun
luminated the gods within the
anctuary as they had done for
ree thousand years. Despite
verything, Ramses II and his
rchitectural masterpiece continue
o survive.

© UNESCO/Nenadovic

OT ONLY ABU SIMBEL

he structure of the High Dam at
swan is 3,600 metres long and
11 high. The lake that it created
as almost 500 kilometres in
ength, 180 of which were in Sudan.
his artificial basin brought about a
adical change within the
nvironment and landscape,
cluding the evacuation of many
ubian villages that lay within the

area of the basin. As soon as it was
realised that the planned
improvement in Egypt's economic
situation entailed the inevitable
destruction of its archaeological
heritage, UNESCO took up the
appeal launched by the
governments of Egypt and Sudan
and undertook an immense
campaign to collect the funds

necessary to save the temples
under threat. In return, Egypt would
donate half of the material
excavated and four of the temples
saved. None of the fifteen
monuments included in the
operation was preserved in its
original location. Only the temple of
Gerf Hussein could not be saved
due to the extreme brittleness of the

© UNESCO/Nenadovic

© UNESCO/Nenadovic

rock. The other fourteen were a[l] dismantled and faithfully reconstructed, ten located near their original sites (Kalabsha, Qertas, Beit el-Wadi, Wadi es-Sebua, Dakka, Maharraqa, Amada, Derr, Ab[u] Simbel and Abu Oda) and four were donated to the countries tha[t] had done most t[o] rescue them: El-Lesiya to Italy, Taffeh to the Netherlands, Dendur to the United States an[d] Dabod to Spain.